Corporate Finance
Made Simple

Corporate Finance Explained
in 100 Pages or Less

Corporate Finance Made Simple

Corporate Finance Explained in 100 Pages or Less

Mike Piper

Dedication

For you, the reader. I hope that the study of finance provides you with useful tools for making good decisions—both in the field of business and in your own personal finances.

Why is there a light bulb on the cover?

In cartoons and comics, a light bulb is often used to signify a moment of clarity or sudden understanding—an "aha!" moment. My hope is that the books in the ...*in 100 Pages or Less* series can help readers achieve clarity and understanding of topics that are often considered complex and confusing—hence the light bulb.

Disclaimer

This book is not intended to be a substitute for personalized advice from a professional financial planner. Nothing contained within this text should be construed as financial advice. The publisher and author make no representation or warranty as to this book's adequacy or appropriateness for any purpose. Similarly, no representation or warranty is made as to the accuracy of the material in this book.

     Purchasing this book does not create any client relationship or other advisory, fiduciary, or professional services relationship with the publisher or with the author. *You alone* bear the *sole* responsibility of assessing the merits and risks associated with any financial decisions you make. And it should always be kept in mind that any investment can result in partial or complete loss.

Your Feedback Is Appreciated!

As the author of this book, I'm very interested to hear your thoughts. If you find the book helpful, please let me know! Alternatively, if you have any suggestions of ways to make the book better, I'm eager to hear that, too.

Finally, if you're dissatisfied with your purchase for any reason, let me know, and I'll be happy to provide you with a refund of the current list price of the book (limited to one refund per household).

You can reach me at: mike@simplesubjects.com.

Best Regards,
Mike Piper, CPA

Table of Contents

Part Three
The Investor's Perspective

Introduction

As with the other books in the *...in 100 Pages or Less* series, this book is written with two assumptions in mind:

a) You want to gain a basic understanding of the book's topic (corporate finance), and
b) You want to achieve that basic level of understanding as quickly as possible.

Given this book's goal of serving as a concise introduction rather than a comprehensive, in-depth text, some decisions had to be made about which topics to include and which topics to discuss most thoroughly. Ultimately, I chose to give particular emphasis to topics that also happen to play important roles in *personal* finance (e.g., the concept of net present value), though, to be clear, this is still very much a book about corporate finance.

And in service of the same goal, certain topics have been omitted if it's very likely that you have already learned about them elsewhere. For instance, we won't be discussing the purpose of a balance sheet or income statement, nor will we be discussing the calculation of most financial ratios, as you will already be familiar with that subject matter if you have taken an accounting course or read any books about accounting. (In case you do want to learn about financial ratios, the relevant chapter from my book *Accounting Made Simple* has been provided as an excerpt at the end of this book, as an appendix.)

What is Corporate Finance?

Corporate finance is primarily concerned with two broad topics: how businesses *access* capital (i.e., money) to fund their operations and how businesses choose to *use* the capital that they have.[1]

    There are two basic ways in which a business can raise capital. It can borrow money, or the existing owners can sell a share of the business. We will discuss the pros and cons of each option—and how a business can find a balance between the two—in Part 1 of this book.

    In Part 2 of the book, we will discuss capital budgeting, which is the process of evaluating potential projects or investments (i.e., potential ways in which a business can *use* its limited capital).

    In Part 3, we will discuss valuation of the two most fundamental financial instruments: stocks and bonds. Note that this is closely related to the topics from Part 1, except that now we will be looking from the perspective of the investor (i.e., the party *providing* the capital).

---

[1] While corporate finance naturally focuses on corporations, many of the concepts still apply to other types of businesses, such as partnerships or LLCs.

Finance and Accounting

If you've taken any accounting courses, you know that the purpose of accounting is largely to provide internal and external users with financial information about a business—whether in the form of financial statements or other reports. Finance is one field that *uses* that information. A business's finance professionals are constantly looking at the business's own financial information to make decisions such as whether to pay a dividend to shareholders, whether to pay down debt, whether to borrow more money, and so on. And in many cases financial professionals will look at financial statements of other businesses as well (e.g., to evaluate whether their firm should acquire the other business).

One difference between accounting and finance is that accounting is primarily concerned with recording and reporting events that have already happened, whereas finance is primarily concerned with making projections and plans about the future.

Another key distinction between accounting and finance is that, in finance, we are not required to follow any specific set of official rules (such as Generally Accepted Accounting Principles or International Financial Reporting Standards that must be followed in accounting). We are instead free to use whatever calculation methods we want, in order to get the necessary information to make the decisions we have to make.

3

PART ONE

Raising Capital

CHAPTER ONE

Raising Capital by Borrowing

The simplest way for a business to raise capital is by borrowing. Sometimes this is done by taking out a loan with a bank (or other lender, such as an insurance company or, in some cases, the federal government).

Other times, firms borrow by issuing (i.e., creating and selling) bonds to investors in exchange for cash. A bond is essentially an IOU. Investors buy the bonds from the issuer, and in exchange the issuer agrees to pay back the principal at a later date known as the maturity date, as well as make specified interest payments (e.g., every 6 months) to the owner of the bond until the bond matures.

Bond Terminology

The "par value" of a bond (also referred to as the bond's "face value") is the value that the borrower must pay back upon maturity, and it is also the value upon which the interest payments are calculated.

The bond's "coupon rate" is the rate used to calculate the periodic interest payments. Specifically, the interest paid per year will be equal to the bond's par value, multiplied by the bond's coupon rate.

EXAMPLE: Medical Manufacturing needs to raise $10 million for a planned expansion. The firm decides to raise the capital by issuing bonds. The bonds will have a $1,000 par value, a 5% coupon rate, and a 10-year term to maturity. The bonds will pay interest annually.

If the bonds sell for their par value, Medical Manufacturing will have to sell 10,000 bonds (i.e., $10 million ÷ $1,000 per bond) in order to raise the desired capital. I say "*if* the bonds sell for their par value" because bonds often sell for somewhat more or less than par value. But don't worry about that for now. We'll discuss this point more thoroughly in Chapter 9, when we discuss bonds from the standpoint of the investor.

Medical Manufacturing will pay $50 interest (i.e., 5% coupon rate multiplied by the $1,000 par value) to each bondholder every year, until the bonds mature. The firm will also pay $1,000 to each bondholder on the maturity date, 10 years from when the bonds are issued.

Cost of Borrowing

The cost of borrowing is the interest that the company has to pay to its lenders. The rate of interest that a firm would have to pay on new debt depends on factors such as:

- The credit rating of the company. That is, how likely is the company to default on the debt? The more likely, the higher the interest rate.
- The term of the bonds or loan. Long-term debt generally has higher interest rates than short-term debt, because it is riskier to the lender.[1]
- Market interest rates (i.e., the interest rates currently being paid on other bonds with similar duration and credit rating).

---

[1] There are a few reasons why long-term debt is riskier to the investor than short-term debt. A longer maturity means there is more time for a default to occur. A longer maturity means there is a greater risk of inflation significantly damaging the value of the interest payments and principal repayment. And a longer maturity means that the bond's price will be more volatile. We'll discuss this risk more thoroughly in Chapter 9.

- Whether the debt is secured or unsecured. With secured debt, the borrower pledges specific assets as collateral for the loan. If the borrower defaults, the lender can seize those assets and sell them in order to recoup their loss. With unsecured debt, no collateral is pledged; the lender is simply relying on the borrower's creditworthiness. Given its riskier nature, unsecured debt generally has a higher interest rate than secured debt.

Often a company can estimate the rate of interest they would have to pay on a new bond issue by looking at the current interest rate (specifically, the yield to maturity—a concept we'll discuss more thoroughly in Chapter 9) on outstanding bonds of a similar duration issued by other companies with similar credit ratings.

One additional point to note here is that, as a company depends more and more heavily on debt, it becomes a higher risk to lenders (i.e., the company has a higher risk of defaulting). As a result, the more debt a firm has, the higher the interest rate it will have to pay for additional borrowing.

Risk of Borrowing

A primary downside of financing via debt is that it is *risky*. A firm cannot simply choose not to pay back its lenders in periods when sales are bad. Outside of bankruptcy, the firm is legally on the hook for the principal and interest owed. (In contrast, if a firm raises capital by selling equity, the new shareholders simply share in the business's losses during unprofitable periods. That is, the new owners share the risk.)

Chapter 1 Simple Summary

- A company can raise capital by borrowing—sometimes by taking out a large loan with a lender such as a bank, or sometimes by issuing bonds to the public.

- The cost of financing via borrowing is the interest paid.

- The interest rate a company will have to pay on new borrowing depends on the company's credit rating, whether the debt is secured or unsecured, the term of the loan, and current market interest rates.

- Borrowing is a source of risk to a firm. Even in unprofitable periods for the firm, its lenders will still demand timely repayment.

CHAPTER TWO

Raising Capital by Selling Equity

Aside from borrowing, the primary way a business can raise capital is by selling equity (i.e., selling a share of ownership of the firm).

Common Stock

The way a firm sells equity is by issuing (i.e., creating and selling) new shares of stock in exchange for cash. There are two types of stock that a corporation might issue: common stock and preferred stock. We will discuss preferred stock later in this chapter.

Common stock is what most people think of when they think of a stock. Owning common stock gives a shareholder certain rights with regard to the corporation. Specifically:

- When the corporation makes a dividend payment (i.e., a distribution of profits), that payment goes to the shareholders;
- Shareholders have a right to vote on major matters of corporate policy, including electing members to the board of directors;
- Shareholders have liquidation rights in the event of bankruptcy. That is, they have a claim to any residual assets that remain after lenders have been paid what they are owed. In many bankruptcy cases though, there aren't any residual assets—that's why the firm is bankrupt.
- Shareholders have a right to sue the company for damages caused by mismanagement or wrongful acts by management or the board of directors.
- Shareholders have a right to receive financial reports and financial statements, and to inspect the corporation's financial records.

Cost of Equity

When a firm raises capital by selling equity, existing owners incur a cost as a result of the fact that they will have a smaller portion of each of the rights mentioned above.

EXAMPLE: You and your sister have formed a business (Widgets Incorporated), which manufactures

11

widgets. Each of you currently owns a 50% share of the business.

You collectively decide to sell a 60% share of the firm to a new investor, in exchange for capital that you will use to expand operations.

Now, you and your sister each own only a 20% share of the business (because the new investor owns 60% of the shares, and the two preexisting owners each own half of the other 40%).

Now, if the firm pays a dividend, your family collectively only receives 40% of that dividend.

Or, if Widgets Incorporated is bought out by a larger firm in the industry (e.g., Widgets Megacorp), 60% of that sale price will go to the new investor instead of to you and your sibling.

In addition, the new investor has 60% of the voting power in the company. This means that the new investor can, by himself/herself, outvote you and your sister on any issues on which there is disagreement. The new investor would be said to have a "controlling interest" in the firm, because he/she owns more than half of the voting stock.

The concepts in the above example would still be true if the business in question were a very large corporation with many shareholders. When a corporation issues new shares of stock in exchange for capital, the preexisting shareholders incur a cost, because going forward they will have a smaller share of the ownership rights (i.e., dividend rights, voting rights, etc.).

Preferred Stock

Preferred stock is different from common stock in several ways. First, it does not come with any voting rights. Second, it has a stated par value, much like a bond. Third, preferred stock dividends are a fixed amount (expressed as a percentage of par value). Fourth, preferred shareholders have higher priority than common shareholders with regard to both liquidation and dividends; this is why it's known as "preferred" stock.

With regard to liquidation, this higher priority means that if the firm is liquidated (e.g., in the event of bankruptcy), all preferred shareholders must receive an amount equal to the par value of their preferred shares before any amount can be distributed to common shareholders. (Lenders still come before preferred shareholders in a liquidation though. No shareholders of any type receive anything in liquidation until creditors have been paid.)

With regard to dividends, this higher priority means that dividends cannot be paid to common stockholders unless the necessary dividend has been paid to preferred shareholders for the year.

Just to be clear, a corporation does *not* have to pay dividends to its preferred shareholders each year. But if it wants to pay a dividend to common shareholders, it must first pay the prescribed dividend amount to its preferred shareholders.

EXAMPLE: Medical Manufacturing issues 1 million shares of preferred stock, with a $25 per share par value and a 6% dividend.

Medical Manufacturing does not have to pay dividends to preferred shareholders. But if it wants to pay any dividends to common stockholders, it must first pay the 6% dividend (i.e., $1.50 per share in a given year) for the preferred shares.

Some preferred stock shares are "cumulative," which means that if the corporation does not pay the stated dividend in a given period, the dividend will have to *eventually* be paid before common stock dividends can be paid. The cumulative amount of preferred dividends that have not been paid is known as a "dividend in arrears."

EXAMPLE: Medical Manufacturing has 1 million shares of cumulative preferred stock outstanding. The shares have a $25 per share par value and a 6% dividend (i.e., $1.50 per year).

Medical Manufacturing has not paid any preferred stock dividends in any of the three prior years. The total amount of dividends in arrears is $4.50 per share (i.e., $1.50 x 3 years). If the firm wants to pay any dividends on its common stock this year, it will have to first pay the full amount of dividends in arrears, *as well as* the $1.50 preferred dividend that is due for this year.

If the preferred stock was noncumulative instead, the firm would only have to pay this year's

$1.50 per-share preferred dividend before paying common stock dividends.

In summary, preferred stock has characteristics of both bonds and common stock. It is like a bond, in that it provides the investor with a predictable payment over time (at least, more predictable than common stock dividends), and it does not offer any voting power. But it is like a stock in that it does not mature, and the periodic payments are not mandatory each period.

Private Placements & Venture Capital

For a startup firm, raising capital via equity may be a necessity, given that banks and bond buyers are generally not eager to lend to a firm with no operations and no assets.

Specifically, startup firms often have to raise capital by selling equity through a "private placement." A private placement is a non-public offering of stock (i.e., an offering to a specifically-chosen potential investor or group of such investors).

"Venture capital" is the term for capital provided in exchange for equity in a startup firm. Venture capital can be provided by individual investors or by various other entities (e.g., investment firms organized for just such a purpose).

The goal of venture capital investors is usually for the firm to "go public" (discussed next) or for the firm to get bought out by a larger firm in the industry—either of which would typically provide a significant payday to the existing shareholders.

Going Public

The opposite of a private placement is a "public offering." In a public offering, stock is sold to the public rather than offered directly to a pre-selected group of potential buyers.

The first time a corporation makes a public offering, it is known as an "initial public offering" (IPO). This is often referred to as "going public." The IPO process involves quite a bit of regulation, enforced by the Securities and Exchange Commission (SEC).

After the IPO, the company is "publicly traded," which means that its shares will be freely traded on one or more stock exchanges. That is, anybody with a brokerage account will be able to buy and sell shares of the company.

Publicly traded companies are subject to a variety of ongoing reporting requirements, such as filing public quarterly and annual financial reports and various reports about shareholders who own 5% or more of a given class of stock. These ongoing reporting requirements are also enforced by the SEC.

Primary and Secondary Markets

The initial sale of stock at the IPO (in which the corporation itself is the seller) is known as the "primary market." Buying and selling between various parties on a stock exchange is known as the "secondary market."

This primary/secondary market distinction exists for bonds as well. When bonds are first issued, that's the primary market. When existing bonds are bought and sold, that's the secondary market.

A key point to recognize is that it is only primary market transactions that actually raise capital for the firm. When third parties buy and sell shares (or bonds) amongst themselves on the secondary market, the firm is largely unaffected. (A firm can also buy—and later resell—existing shares of its own stock on the secondary market. But in the vast majority of secondary market transactions, the firm itself is neither the buyer nor seller.)

Chapter 2 Simple Summary

- Aside from borrowing, the primary way in which a business can raise capital is by selling equity (i.e., selling a share of the firm).

- Shareholders of common stock have an assortment of rights, including the right to share in the profits of the firm and the right to vote on major corporate policies.

- When a firm raises capital by selling equity, the cost to pre-existing shareholders comes from the fact that they will now own a smaller share of the business.

- Preferred stock has characteristics of both common stock and bonds. Preferred stock dividends are not guaranteed, but when they are paid, the amount is fixed. Like common stock, preferred stock does not mature. Unlike common stock, preferred stock does not carry voting rights.

- The primary market consists of transactions in which a corporation sells new bonds or new shares of stock, such as in its initial public offering (IPO). In the secondary market, various parties buy and sell existing bonds or existing shares of stock.

CHAPTER THREE

Dividend Policy

In addition to borrowing and selling equity, a firm has access to one more source of capital: its own profits. That is, after earning a profit, a firm has a choice. It can either distribute that profit to shareholders (i.e., pay a dividend), or it can reinvest those profits in the company.

A firm's decisions regarding dividends (i.e., whether to pay dividends and how much to pay) are collectively known as its "dividend policy."

As a general rule, a firm's dividend policy should depend on the rate of return that management thinks it can earn on retained (reinvested) earnings. Specifically, does management think that the company can generate higher returns for a given level of risk than shareholders would be able to generate, if they had the money in their hands? If so, management should reinvest earnings in the company. If not, management should distribute earnings to shareholders, so that they can invest the capital as they see fit.

Often, newer firms pay no dividends because they are not yet earning a profit. And even when they are profitable, newer firms tend to a) have very limited capital and b) have many investment opportunities that they have not yet pursued, so they pay no dividends or very small dividends, choosing instead to use earnings to fund further growth.

Conversely, mature firms are more likely to be profitable. And they are more likely to have limited opportunities for growth. So they tend to pay higher dividends.

EXAMPLE: Carabiner Climbing operates three rock climbing gyms in a midwestern city. Each gym became profitable almost immediately after opening. The firm's management is highly confident that it could open an additional location in a nearby city with similar results.

Because the firm believes it has the opportunity to earn relatively high returns with relatively low risk, it chooses *not* to pay out profits as dividends and to instead use its profits to fund the opening of a new location.

EXAMPLE: Timely Taxes is a tax preparation service, operating nationwide. It has already expanded into the various markets where management believes it can operate profitably. And management is not especially optimistic about any plans to expand into offering new products/services.

Because the firm does not see any especially attractive opportunities for reinvesting earnings, it chooses to pay out a majority of earnings as dividends to shareholders.

Dividend Dates

There are a few dates that are important with respect to a firm paying a dividend.

The "declaration date" is the date on which the firm declares (announces) the upcoming dividend payment.

The "date of record" is the date by which a person (or other entity) must be in the company's records as a shareholder in order to receive the dividend in question.

However, it takes some time for a stock trade to be finalized and for records to be updated. Therefore, in order for an investor to be on the list of shareholders as of the date of record, they would have to have purchased the stock somewhat prior to the date of record. Specifically, they would have to purchase the stock before the "ex-dividend date."

The "ex-dividend date" is generally one business day *before* the date of record. The ex-dividend date is the date on which the stock is said to be trading "ex-dividend" (i.e., without a dividend). That is, if an investor purchases the stock on the ex-dividend date or after, they would not get the dividend in question. In contrast, if they bought it on the day before the ex-dividend date, they would receive the dividend.

Because an investor who buys before the ex-dividend date *would* be entitled to the dividend while an investor who buys on or after the ex-dividend date would *not* be entitled to the dividend, the firm's share price generally drops by roughly the amount of the dividend on the ex-dividend date.

The "date of payment" is exactly what it sounds like: the date on which the dividend payment is actually sent to the appropriate recipients.

EXAMPLE: On Tuesday March 19, a corporation declares a dividend payment. The dividend will be paid on Tuesday April 9, to shareholders of record as of Wednesday March 27.

In this example, March 19 is the declaration date. March 27 is the date of record. April 9 is the date of payment. The ex-dividend date will be Tuesday March 26, because that is the business day prior to the date of record. If a person purchases a share of the stock on or after March 26, they will not receive the dividend payment in question.

Stock Repurchases

When a firm believes that it has excess capital relative to its attractive investment opportunities, paying a dividend is one way to return capital to shareholders. Another option is to institute a stock buyback (i.e., use cash to buy shares from existing shareholders).

When a firm repurchases its own shares, the remaining shareholders each now own a larger share of the company. (It's essentially the opposite of what happens when new shares are issued.)

In some cases when a firm buys stock back from shareholders the shares are canceled completely. In other cases, the firm simply holds the stock—often with the intention of reselling it on the secondary market at a later time (e.g., when additional capital is needed). When a firm owns its own stock in this way, the shares are known as "treasury stock."

One advantage of a stock buyback relative to paying a dividend is that it is more tax-efficient from the perspective of the shareholder. That is, with a stock repurchase, it is only the shareholders who *choose* to sell their shares who will have to pay any income tax—and, even for them, there may not be a tax cost (if the shares were sold at a loss for example). With a dividend, every shareholder receives the dividend and has to pay any associated income tax.

Another advantage of stock repurchases (relative to paying dividends) is that the firm has somewhat more flexibility. The firm can repurchase many shares in one period—and then few or no shares in the following period—with little or no adverse consequences. In contrast, if a firm with a history of paying a steady dividend suddenly cuts its dividend, shareholders tend to be unhappy, and the market price of the stock tends to fall.

Chapter 3 Simple Summary

- Other than borrowing and selling equity, a firm has access to one more source of capital: its own profits. Earnings that are not distributed to shareholders can be reinvested in the company.

- A firm's decisions about whether to reinvest earnings or distribute them as a dividend are known as the firm's "dividend policy."

- Dividend policy generally depends on the firm's capital needs and on the rate of return that management thinks it can earn on reinvested earnings. If management thinks it can earn a higher rate of return for a given level of risk than is available elsewhere, it should retain the earnings rather than distribute them. (As a result, newer firms—with more untapped opportunities for growth—often do not pay dividends.)

- As an alternative to paying a dividend, a stock repurchase is another way to distribute unneeded capital to shareholders.

CHAPTER FOUR

Capital Structure

A business will typically fund its needs with debt and with equity (either by selling equity to raise cash or by reinvesting its own earnings). *How much* of the business is funded with debt and how much with equity—and what type(s) of debt and what type(s) of equity—is known as the firm's "capital structure."

Debt-to-Equity Ratio

A common measure of a firm's capital structure is the firm's "debt-to-equity ratio." This ratio is calculated as the sum of all of the firm's debt (liability) accounts from the balance sheet, divided by the sum of all of the firm's equity accounts from the balance sheet.[1]

$$\text{debt-to-equity ratio} = \frac{\text{total debt}}{\text{total equity}}$$

EXAMPLE: Capital Contracting's balance sheet can be seen on the following page. What is the firm's debt-to-equity ratio?

In this case, the firm's total debt is $240,000, and the firm's total equity is $160,000. So the firm's debt-to-equity ratio is 1.5, calculated as $240,000 ÷ $160,000.

---

[1] Sometimes the debt-to-equity ratio is calculated using only long-term debt balances. Also, the ratio is sometimes calculated using market values instead of accounting/book values.

Balance Sheet

Assets

Cash and Cash Equivalents	$40,000
Inventory	$110,000
Property, Plant, and Equipment	$250,000
Total Assets	$400,000

Liabilities

Notes Payable	$240,000
Total Liabilities	$240,000

Owners' Equity

Common Stock	$50,000
Retained Earnings	$110,000
Total Owners' Equity	$160,000
Total Liabilities + Owners' Equity	$400,000

A firm's decisions about capital structure are primarily influenced by two things: risk and cost.

Risk

For two reasons, financing via debt is riskier than financing via equity.

Firstly, if the corporation does not make payments on time, it can result in additional interest, fees, legal costs, and potentially even bankruptcy. By contrast, equity does not result in any legal obligation to pay anybody. If a firm goes through an unprofitable period, it can simply choose not to pay any dividends. It cannot choose not to make debt payments—not without facing expensive consequences, anyway.

The second reason that it is risky to use debt has to do with a concept known as "financial leverage." A lever can be used to lift a large object with relatively little force. That is, it magnifies the force you can apply. The use of debt in a firm's capital structure is known as financial leverage because it has a similar magnification effect—making profitable firms more profitable and making unprofitable firms more unprofitable.

Why does using debt (financial leverage) magnify a firm's results? The more capital a business uses, the more operations it can fund (e.g., more product lines, more retail locations, etc.). And when the firm has a larger level of operations, it has greater potential for larger profits or losses. When a firm borrows, it increases its capital *without requiring the owners to invest more of their own capital*. As a result, the firm can fund a larger level of operations (and thereby achieve a larger level of profits or losses) for a given level of shareholder capital (i.e., equity). In short, financing via borrowing magnifies the return on the owners' own capital—whether those returns are positive or negative.

Cost of Capital

So if financing via debt is riskier than financing via equity, why do firms often include debt in their capital structure? In short, because it's less expensive (up to a point).

As discussed in Chapter 1, capital raised via debt has a cost because the firm will have to pay interest on that debt. And as discussed in Chapter 2, capital raised by selling equity has a cost because it means that part of the firm's profit will go to new owners.

The cost of debt is usually lower than the cost of equity for two reasons.

The first reason that financing via debt is usually less expensive than financing via equity has to do with taxes. Specifically, interest paid on debt is generally deductible to the corporation, whereas equity costs (i.e., profits that go to the new owners instead of preexisting owners) are not deductible.

The second reason has to do with the perspective of the investor (i.e., the party *supplying* capital to the firm). The cash flows that are cost of capital to the firm (i.e., interest payments on debt or dividend payments to new shareholders) are *return* to the investor. From the perspective of the investor, debt is safer than equity. With debt, the investor knows what return they will get (i.e., the interest rate, assuming there is no default). With equity, the investor's return is much less predictable. So investors will generally only want to supply capital in exchange for equity if they *expect* to receive a higher return than they would earn by lending capital to the firm. That is, investors generally demand a higher return (higher cost of capital to the firm) for equity than for debt.

However, as a firm borrows more and more, its cost of debt rises. That is, potential lenders will recognize that the firm has a higher risk of defaulting, due to its high level of existing indebtedness. And they will therefore charge the firm a higher interest rate for any new borrowing. This is why financing via debt is only less expensive "up to a point." That is, there comes a point at which the firm will be so heavily indebted that future borrowing will significantly drive up the firm's cost of capital.[1]

Point being, it's a balance. The ideal debt-to-equity ratio will depend on the specifics of the firm and the industry. All else being equal though, the riskier the firm's operations, the less risk it should take on via borrowing. For example, if a firm has very volatile sales from year to year, it likely would do well to finance primarily via equity rather than debt. If it financed primarily via debt, it might have a hard time meeting its obligations in some years.

---

[1] As the firm becomes heavily indebted, it is not only the cost of debt (borrowing) that increases, the cost of equity increases as well, as equity investors will demand a higher rate of return for investing in a distressed firm.

Calculating Cost of Capital

A firm shouldn't pay for access to capital unless it expects to earn a higher return than the cost that it is paying for that capital. In the same line of thinking, a firm shouldn't use capital on a new project unless it expects the returns from that project to exceed the applicable cost of capital.

To be able to make such decisions, a firm must be able to *calculate* its cost of capital. Financial managers are often interested in the firm's "weighted average cost of capital" (WACC). A firm's weighted average cost of capital is the firm's cost of capital (expressed as a percentage), when we take into account how much of the firm's capital structure is debt and how much is equity.

Consider this (hopefully intuitive) example: A firm has a capital structure that is half debt and half equity. If the firm has an 8% cost of debt and 12% cost of equity, the firm's weighted average cost of capital would be 10%.

Here's the actual equation we use to calculate weighted average cost of capital:

$$\text{WACC} = \left(\frac{D}{D+E} \times C_D \right) + \left(\frac{E}{D+E} \times C_E \right)$$

...where D is the total market value of the firm's debt, E is the total market value of the firm's equity, C_D is the after-tax cost of debt (expressed as a percentage), and C_E is the cost of equity (expressed as a percentage).[1]

In short, we're multiplying the firm's cost of debt (C_D) by the portion of the firm that is financed by debt [D / (D+E)]. And we are multiplying the firm's cost of equity (C_E) by the portion of the firm that is financed via equity [E / (D+E)]. That's why it's a *weighted average* cost of capital.

EXAMPLE: Widgets, Inc. has an after-tax cost of debt of 7% and cost of equity of 13%. The market value of the firm's debt is $1 million, and the market value of the firm's equity is $2 million. What is Widgets, Inc's weighted average cost of capital?

We turn to our equation:

$$\text{WACC} = \left(\frac{D}{D + E} \times C_D \right) + \left(\frac{E}{D + E} \times C_E \right)$$

---

[1] There are two important points to note here.

One: we use market value rather than "book value" (i.e., accounting values from financial statements) because we are concerned with forward looking analysis here, so we want today's values rather than just historical amounts.

Two: in this equation we are assuming that the firm has no preferred stock. If the firm's capital structure does include preferred stock, the equation would include a separate term (i.e., another piece of addition) for that. That is, we would also add the firm's cost of preferred stock, multiplied by the percentage of the firm's capital structure that is made up of preferred stock.

In this case, the firm's total market value of debt and equity is $3 million. So the weight of debt is $1 million ÷ $3 million, or 1/3. And the weight of equity is $2 million ÷ $3 million, or 2/3.

WACC = (1/3 x 7%) + (2/3 x 13%) = 11%

Where does a firm get the numbers to plug into this equation?

A firm's cost of debt can be observed directly: it's the after-tax interest rate the company would have to pay on new borrowing. For example, if the company would have to pay a 10% interest rate for a new bank loan or a new bond issue, and the company has a 30% tax rate, the firm's cost of debt would be 7% (because the firm would be getting a tax deduction with a value of 30% of the 10% interest, or 3%).

For preferred stock, the cost is simply the dividend payment (in dollars) divided by the current market price of a share of preferred stock.

For common stock, the cost is the total return investors demand (i.e., dividends plus price appreciation). But this amount is trickier to determine. We can only estimate it, using various assumptions and methods (such as the capital asset pricing model, which we'll discuss in Chapter 10).

A key point here is that whether we're talking about cost of debt or cost of equity, it is the investors (i.e., the *providers* of capital) who set the cost. The firm must know what its cost of capital is and make decisions—about both raising capital and using capital—accordingly.

Chapter 4 Simple Summary

- A firm's capital structure refers to how much of the business is funded via debt and how much is funded via equity.

- A firm's debt-to-equity ratio is a common metric of capital structure. It is calculated as the sum of all of the firm's debt (liability) accounts from the balance sheet, divided by the sum of all of the firm's equity accounts from the balance sheet. (Sometimes the debt-to-equity ratio is calculated using only long-term debt balances. And sometimes it is calculated using market values instead of accounting/book values.)

- Capital structure decisions involve a balance between cost and risk. Raising capital via debt is generally less expensive than raising capital via equity (up to a point), but debt carries more risk, as it results in a contractual obligation to pay.

- A firm's weighted average cost of capital is the firm's cost of capital, when we take into account how much of the firm's capital structure is debt and how much is equity.

PART TWO

Deploying Capital: Capital Budgeting

CHAPTER FIVE

Evaluating a Project: Forecasting Cash Flows

"Capital budgeting" is the process of evaluating potential projects or investments (i.e., potential ways in which a business can *use* its capital). Capital budgeting is normally focused on major or long-term projects. (A business would not, for instance, bother with a capital budgeting process to determine whether to purchase new office supplies.)

In capital budgeting we are concerned with determining which projects/investments to accept (i.e., pursue) and which ones to reject. In most cases, the goal is to use capital in the way that is projected to maximize the value of the firm. A critical step in evaluating a project is to forecast the cash flows that would result from that project—both the cash *outflows* that will pay for the project and the *inflows* that are hoped to result from the project.

Which Cash Flows Are Relevant?

A key point in forecasting cash flows is that we only want to consider marginal/incremental cash flows (i.e., the amount by which the firm's cash flows will *change* as a result of the project).

EXAMPLE: MTB Manufacturing is considering a major research and development initiative to create a new mountain bike product line. MTB expects annual sales to be $1.7 million per year over the next several years if they do not proceed with the project, or $2 million per year if they do proceed with the project. In this case, the relevant cash inflow for the project would *not* be $2 million per year. Rather, it would be $300,000 per year (i.e., the amount by which cash flow would *change* as a result of the project).

A related point is that we always want to exclude "sunk costs" (i.e., money that has already been spent) from the analysis.

EXAMPLE: Last year, MTB Manufacturing spent $500,000 toward developing a new product line. MTB had anticipated that the new product would be ready by this point, but the project has not made as much progress as anticipated. The firm now expects that an additional $400,000 would be necessary to complete development for the new product.

When evaluating whether to continue with the project, the $500,000 that has already been spent is a sunk cost and should *not* be included in the analysis. It is only the remaining $400,000 of projected costs that should be weighed against the anticipated inflows for the project.

In some cases, the cash flow from a project isn't actually a cash inflow, but rather a reduction in outflow—but we treat it as a cash inflow anyway. For example, purchasing a new piece of equipment to replace old, unreliable equipment might be expected to result in lower annual maintenance costs. That reduction in annual maintenance costs would be included as a cash inflow for the project.

After-Tax Cash Flows

In all cases, we want to look at *after-tax* cash flows, because that's what would actually be made available to shareholders.

For operating cash flows from a project (i.e., ongoing cash inflows and outflows) we multiply the pre-tax cash flow by 1 minus the firm's marginal tax rate. For example, if a firm has a 30% marginal tax rate, we would multiply by $(1 - 0.3)$, or 70%, because the firm only gets to keep 70% of the cash flows in question.

In many cases, the initial outlay from a project is included in a cash flow analysis at its full value, because the initial outlay is often not deductible. For example, if a firm is considering purchasing a new piece of equipment or a new building, such expenditures are (in many cases) not immediately deductible. Instead, the firm will claim depreciation deductions over several years. (Essentially, the cost of the equipment or building is deducted over time rather than all at once.)

For such purchases, the full cost of the initial outlay would be included in the cash flow analysis. And then the tax savings that occur each year as a result of the depreciation would be included in the analysis as a cash inflow (i.e., a reduction in the tax outflow each year). In other words, depreciation itself is not a cash flow, but it results in a tax reduction, which *is* a cash flow.

To summarize:

- We always want to look at after-tax cash flows when evaluating a project.
- To adjust pre-tax operating cash flows to after-tax, we multiply by [1 - tax rate].
- The initial outlay for a project/investment is included at face value (i.e., there is no tax adjustment) if it is not deductible.
- The annual cash flow (i.e., tax savings) from depreciation is calculated as [annual depreciation deduction x tax rate].

EXAMPLE: MTB Manufacturing is considering purchasing a piece of equipment. The equipment is projected to cost $100,000, and it will be depreciated for tax purposes on a straight-line basis over 5 years (i.e., $20,000 deduction per year). The equipment is expected to result in pre-tax operating inflows of $50,000 per year for 5 years. MTB's tax rate is 30%.

Find the after-tax cash flow over the first year (including the initial outlay).

	Pre-Tax	Tax Effect	After-Tax
Initial outlay	($100,000)	n/a	($100,000)
Operating inflow	$50,000	($15,000)	$35,000
Depreciation	n/a	$6,000	$6,000
Net cash flow	($50,000)		($59,000)

The after-tax cash flow for the first year of the project will be a $59,000 outflow. That is, a $100,000 outflow from the initial outlay, netted against a $35,000 after-tax operating cash inflow and a $6,000 cash inflow from the tax savings from the $20,000 depreciation deduction.

Chapter 5 Simple Summary

- A critical step in capital budgeting is to forecast the cash flows that will result from an investment/project.

- When evaluating a project, we are only concerned with the extent to which cash flows will *change* as a result of the project.

- When evaluating a project, we do not want to include sunk costs (i.e., costs that have already been incurred) in the analysis.

- In capital budgeting, we care about after-tax cash flows, rather than before-tax cash flows.

CHAPTER SIX

Time Value of Money: *Discounted* Cash Flows

When evaluating a project, we care not only *how much* cash flow is expected, we also care *when* those cash flows will be received.

For example, consider the following two projects.

	Project A	**Project B**
Initial outlay	($200,000)	($200,000)
Year 1	$0	$300,000
Year 2	$0	$200,000
Year 3	$200,000	$0
Year 4	$300,000	$0
Net cash flow	$300,000	$300,000

Each project has the same initial cost. And each has a forecasted total net cash flow of $300,000. But there's a big difference in timing. Project B provides its cash flow sooner. All else being equal, we'd rather get our money sooner rather than later.

This leads us to a discussion of perhaps the most important principle in all of finance: "time value of money."

The concept of time value of money is something that people know intuitively: given the choice between a dollar today or a dollar at some specific point in the future, you would rather have the dollar today.

One reason for this preference is inflation. That is, a dollar in the future will likely purchase somewhat less than a dollar would purchase today.

But even if you somehow knew that there would be no inflation, you would *still* prefer to receive a dollar today than a dollar, say, one year from now. Why not, right? If nothing else, you could invest it over the year in question and end up with more than one dollar by the end of the year.

And that's the second reason that a dollar today is worth more than a dollar in the future. The sooner you receive a given cash flow, the sooner you can begin to earn a return on that cash.

Future Value

The "future value" of an asset is the amount that the asset will be worth at some specific point in the future, given a particular rate of return.

EXAMPLE: You purchase a $1,000 1-year CD, which has a 2% interest rate. What is the future value of the CD (i.e., its value when it matures one year from now)?

$1,000 x 1.02 = $1,020.

The future value of $1,000, invested at a 2% return for one year is $1,020. The CD will be worth $1,020 when it matures.

EXAMPLE: You purchase a $1,000 3-year CD, which has a 2% interest rate. What is the future value of the CD three years from now?

$1,000 x 1.02 x 1.02 x 1.02 = $1,061.21

Or more succinctly: $1,000 x $(1.02)^3$ = $1,061.21

Or to put it more broadly:

$FV = PV \times (1 + r)^n$

where:

- FV is future value,
- PV is present value,
- r is the rate of return (as a decimal), and
- n is the number of periods.

Present Value

"Present value" is essentially the inverse concept of future value. With future value, we have a given amount of money today, and we want to know how much it will be worth at a specified date in the future, given a specified rate of return.

With present value, we want to know how much a future cash flow is worth today.

EXAMPLE: You have the option to purchase a bond that would cost $9,000. The bond will provide no interest payments, but it will mature exactly one year from now, at which point it will pay you $10,000. Should you buy this bond?

To answer that question, we have to determine the present value of the $10,000 future cash flow. That is, what is the value *today* of $10,000 one year from now? Is it worth more or less than the $9,000 that you would have to spend on the bond?

To calculate the present value of a future cash flow, we use the following equation:

$$PV = \frac{FV}{(1 + r)^n}$$

where, again:

- FV is future value,
- PV is present value,
- r is the rate of return (as a decimal), and

- n is the number of periods.

In this case, the rate of return that we use is the rate of return that you could earn via other investments with a similar level of risk. This rate of return is known as the "discount rate."

EXAMPLE (continued): You are considering purchasing a bond for $9,000, which is expected to provide a cash flow of $10,000 exactly one year from now. You have other similarly-risky investments available to you, which would be expected to earn a 7% return. How much should you be willing to spend on this bond? (That is, what is the present value of the $10,000 future cash flow?)
    We use our equation from above:

$$PV = \frac{FV}{(1 + r)^n}$$

$$PV = \frac{\$10,000}{(1 + 0.07)^1}$$

PV = $9,346

The present value of the $10,000 future cash flow is $9,346. What this tells us is that if you invested in the *other* available investments (i.e., the ones earning 7% per year—the discount rate), it would require $9,346 in order to return $10,000 one year from now. You should, therefore, be willing to spend *up to* $9,346 on this bond.

Because this bond only costs $9,000, you should likely buy this bond (assuming you have sufficient capital).

Here's another way to think of it: the bond in question costs $9,000. And you know that you can earn a 7% rate of return on other investments with the same amount of risk. If you invested that $9,000 in those other investments, after one year they would be worth $9,630 (that is, $9,000 x 1.07). That's not as good as the bond in question, because it would return $10,000.

If the bond instead cost more than $9,346 (i.e., if its cost were greater than its present value), then you should not buy this bond. You should invest in the other investments instead.

Why Is It Called a Discount Rate?

When we calculate the present value of a future cash flow, we are said to be "discounting" that cash flow (because we are accounting for the fact that a dollar received in the future should not count for as much as a dollar received today—it should be *discounted*). That's why the rate of return that is used in the calculation is known as a "discount rate."

Also, you will sometimes see a present value referred to as a "discounted value."

Key Present Value Takeaways

A critical takeaway about present value is that the further in the future a cash flow will be received, the lower the present value. This should make sense intuitively. Would you rather receive $1,000 two years from now or $1,000 three years from now? Easy decision: sooner is better. And the math works out accordingly.

EXAMPLE: Investment A will provide a $1,000 cash flow two years from now. Investment B will provide a $1,000 cash flow three years from now. You have other available investment opportunities with a similar level of risk that are expected to earn an 8% return. What are the present values of Investment A and of Investment B?

$$PV = \frac{FV}{(1 + r)^n}$$

$$PV \text{ of Investment A} = \frac{\$1,000}{(1.08)^2}$$

PV of Investment A = $857

$$PV \text{ of Investment B} = \frac{\$1,000}{(1.08)^3}$$

PV of Investment B = $794

As expected, the present value of Investment B is lower, because the cash flow occurs further in the future.

Another key takeaway regarding present value is that the higher the discount rate used, the lower the present value.

EXAMPLE: Investment C will provide a $1,000 cash flow two years from now. You have other available investment opportunities with a similar level of risk that are expected to earn an 8% return. What is the present value of Investment C? What would be the present value of Investment C if the comparably-risky investment opportunities were expected to earn 11% instead of 8%?

$$PV = \frac{FV}{(1 + r)^n}$$

$$PV \text{ of Investment C} = \frac{\$1,000}{(1.08)^2}$$

PV of Investment C = $857

And with an 11% discount rate...

$$PV \text{ of Investment C} = \frac{\$1,000}{(1.11)^2}$$

PV of Investment C = $812

As expected, the higher discount rate leads to a lower present value. Point being, the higher the rate of return we're missing out on as we wait for this cash flow, the less enthusiastic we are about buying this investment (i.e., the less we're willing to pay for it). Or stated differently, the better our other available investment options, the less valuable this investment option.[1]

When calculating present value, we always use a discount rate that's based on the risk level of the cash flow in question. The less certain the cash flow, the higher the risk and the higher the discount rate.

And that leads us to a third and final key takeaway about present value: higher risk means higher discount rate, which means lower present value. And while these terms might be new to you, this concept should be another one that makes intuitive sense. After all, which would you rather have: a guaranteed $1,000 cash flow 10 years from now, or a speculative $1,000 cash flow 10 years from now? You would prefer the guaranteed cash flow. The more reliable a future cash flow, the more

---

[1] For readers familiar with economics concepts, you may recognize that this feels a lot like the concept of "opportunity cost." And indeed, that's exactly what it is. The discount rate is essentially your opportunity cost for capital—it's what you could be earning elsewhere with this money (i.e., the return from other comparably-risky investments, that you are giving up in order to purchase this investment).

valuable it is. The less reliable a future cash flow (i.e., the higher the risk), the less valuable it is. That's why we use higher discount rates for riskier cash flows.

Chapter 6 Simple Summary

- Time value of money is the concept that a dollar in the future is worth less than a dollar today.

- The future value of an asset is the amount that the asset will be worth at a specific point in the future, given a specific rate of return.

- The present value of a future cash flow is the amount that that future cash flow is worth to-day.

- When we calculate the present value of a future cash flow, we are said to be "discounting" that cash flow (to reflect the fact that it's worth less than its face value, because it will be received in the future). As a result, the rate of return used in a present value calculation is known as the discount rate.

- The higher the risk of a given cash flow, the higher the appropriate discount rate, and, therefore, the lower the present value.

CHAPTER SEVEN

Net Present Value

Having discussed the concept of time value of money, how do we use that concept in order to determine whether a project is worth pursuing?

In short, we calculate the "net present value" (NPV) of the project. The net present value of an investment is the sum of the present values of each of the cash inflows, minus the sum of the present values of each of the cash outflows.

EXAMPLE: Ruby Research is considering a project that will require an $80,000 initial outlay and which is expected to provide $50,000 cash inflow per year for four years. (Assume these figures are already on an after-tax basis.) What is the NPV of the project, using a 7% discount rate?

To calculate the NPV, we would calculate the present value of each of the cash flows, then sum those present values. The initial outlay occurs immediately, so $80,000 is the present value. (That is, the initial outlay occurs right now, rather than in the future, so we do not need to discount it.) For the inflows, the present value would be calculated as:

$$\text{PV of first year's inflow} = \frac{\$50,000}{(1.07)^1} = \$46,729$$

$$\text{PV of second year's inflow} = \frac{\$50,000}{(1.07)^2} = \$43,672$$

$$\text{PV of third year's inflow} = \frac{\$50,000}{(1.07)^3} = \$40,815$$

$$\text{PV of fourth year's inflow} = \frac{\$50,000}{(1.07)^4} = \$38,145$$

Net present value = -\$80,000 + \$46,729 + \$43,672 + \$40,815 + \$38,145 = \$89,361

As you have likely noticed, calculating NPV by hand can be rather time consuming. And this is just a very simple series of cash flows. In the real world, the projections could extend well beyond four years. And there could be more than one cash flow per year to consider. That's why NPV is most often calculated using Excel or a similar tool.[1]

---

[1] See obliviousinvestor.com/excel-finance/ for a discussion of using Excel to calculate NPV (as well as other related metrics).

Making Decisions Based on NPV

When calculating the NPV of a project, we are asking: does this project add value for shareholders (i.e., does it increase the value of the firm)?

A negative NPV means the project would subtract value (i.e., the cost exceeds the present value of the forecasted cash inflows). When a potential project has a negative NPV, the decision is easy: we reject the project.[1]

A positive NPV means the project would add value for shareholders, which means we would *like* to accept (pursue) the project. And indeed, if a firm had enough capital to pursue all of its positive-NPV potential projects, it *would* pursue all of them.

But most firms have insufficient capital to pursue all of the projects they would like to pursue. In such a case, we rank all of the projects by their respective NPVs. Then we choose the combination of projects that provides the highest total NPV, without exceeding our available capital.

EXAMPLE: Ruby Research has $800,000 of capital available. The initial cost and forecasted NPV for

---

[1] One noteworthy exception occurs when a firm is forced to take on a project with a negative NPV. For instance, if a new piece of regulation requires the firm to meet new environmental standards, the firm would evaluate various ways to achieve that goal. Even if all of the options have a negative NPV, one must still be selected—generally the one with the least-negative NPV.

each of Ruby's potential projects is as follows. Which project(s) should the firm pursue?

	Required Outlay	**NPV**
Project 1	$600,000	$1.8 million
Project 2	$600,000	$1.5 million
Project 3	$300,000	$1.3 million
Project 4	$200,000	$1.1 million

Ruby Research would *like* to pursue all four projects, because each has a positive NPV. But because of the capital limitation, that is not an option.

Ruby should pursue Project 1 and Project 4, because that is the combination that provides the highest total NPV without exceeding the firm's $800,000 capital budget.

In the next chapter, we'll discuss other capital budgeting methods (i.e., other methods for evaluating potential projects). Each method has its pros and cons. But evaluating projects by their net present value (selecting the combination of projects that provides the highest achievable NPV) is generally considered the best method for capital budgeting, because it directly determines the uses of capital that would add the most value for shareholders.

Discount Rate and Risk Level

When doing an NPV calculation, the appropriate discount rate depends on the risk level of the project. Why? Because, as we discussed in the previous chapter, less reliable (higher risk) cash flows are less valuable. So higher risk cash flows need a higher discount rate in order to reflect their lower present value.

Another way to think of it is that we want to make an apples-to-apples comparison. There are always other investment options available, at various levels of risk, via the financial markets. A firm can buy stock of other companies. It can buy a stock market index fund (i.e., a mutual fund that invests in the stock market as a whole). It can buy bonds from other companies. Or it can buy Treasury bonds.

If the project we're evaluating is as risky as, say, the overall stock market, we want to be sure that the project's forecasted return will be at least as good as the forecasted return from the overall stock market. So, when valuing the project, we would use a discount rate equal to the expected return of the stock market, *not* a discount rate that reflects, for instance, Treasury bond interest rates.

An important takeaway here is that determining the risk level of a project is fundamental to determining its NPV. And because there's a fair bit of subjectivity involved in estimating the level of risk—just as there is with forecasting the cash flows themselves—NPV is very much an estimate.

WACC as a Discount Rate

Selecting a discount rate using the approach described so far (i.e., using the expected return from a financial instrument with a similar level of risk to the project being considered) can be tricky—for two reasons.

First, it can be tricky to determine how risky this project is, compared to various financial instruments. For instance, if a local restaurant chain is considering opening a new location, how does the risk level of that project compare to the risk of a stock market index fund? That's not an easy question to answer.

Second, it can be tricky to come up with good estimates of the expected return for certain financial instruments anyway. (There's *a lot* of disagreement about the expected return of the stock market at any given time.)

As such, firms often approach the question of discount rate from another perspective: by considering their cost of capital.

For instance, a firm might be able to confidently say that a project is approximately as risky as the firm's current ongoing operations. (Such might be the case for a project to increase production capacity for an existing product line, for instance.) When the proposed project is approximately as risky as the firm's ongoing operations, the firm's weighted average cost of capital (WACC, discussed in Chapter 4) is an ideal discount rate.

The idea here is to think of the firm itself as a financial instrument. If we know the expected return for that investment, we can use that return as the discount rate for other investments that are similarly risky (i.e., new projects that are approximately as risky as the firm's ongoing operations).

From the perspective of the firm (the party using the capital), cost of capital is a cost. But that same figure is a *return* to the providers of the capital (i.e., interest to bondholders and dividends/capital appreciation to shareholders). That is, a firm's WACC reflects the weighted average *return* to the firm's bondholders and shareholders.

And if WACC is the expected return for investors in the firm, we know that WACC would be a suitable discount rate for investments/projects that are approximately as risky as the firm overall.

If the firm is considering a project that is slightly riskier than the firm's ongoing operations (e.g., a new but related product line), a discount rate slightly higher than the firm's WACC would be appropriate.

If the firm is considering a project that is slightly less risky than its ongoing operations (e.g., installing a new piece of equipment from a reliable manufacturer, to save maintenance costs on an old and unreliable piece of equipment), a discount rate slightly lower than the firm's WACC would be appropriate.

Chapter 7 Simple Summary

- The net present value of an investment is the sum of the present values of the resulting cash flows (netting the inflows against the outflows).

- A positive NPV means that the project would add value to the firm. A negative NPV means the project would subtract value.

- If a firm had sufficient capital to do so, it would accept all projects with a positive NPV. Given limited capital, the best approach is to rank the potential projects by NPV and choose the combination that provides the highest total NPV, without exceeding the firm's capital budget.

- The appropriate discount rate for an NPV calculation depends on the riskiness of the project. In short, the ideal discount rate is the rate of return that the firm could earn on other investments of a similar risk level.

- A firm's weighted average cost of capital is a suitable discount rate for projects that are approximately as risky as the firm's ongoing operations.

CHAPTER EIGHT

Other Capital Budgeting Methods

Calculating a project's net present value is generally considered the best method of evaluating the project, because doing so gets right at the heart of the matter: does this project add value or subtract value for investors? And in either case, *how much* value?

However, other capital budgeting methods are frequently used as well—either because they provide additional information about a project or because they are easier to understand and communicate to others (especially people without a background in finance).

Internal Rate of Return (IRR)

The "internal rate of return" (IRR) for an investment is the discount rate at which the net present value of the cash flows is zero (i.e., it is the discount rate at which the present value of the cash outflows is equal to the present value of the cash inflows). A different and more intuitive way to look at IRR is that it is the expected rate of return for the project.

Don't worry about learning a formula to calculate IRR by hand. Because such an effort would be so time consuming, few people ever do it. Instead, most people use a calculator such as Excel. Such calculators essentially figure it out via trial and error (i.e., starting with a guess as to the rate of return, calculating the resulting NPV using that rate as the discount rate, and then adjusting the discount rate up or down as necessary until NPV = 0).

When we do an IRR calculation for a project, we are concerned with whether the IRR exceeds the "hurdle rate" set by management. The hurdle rate is the minimum rate of return that management has decided is acceptable for a project of this risk level. (The hurdle rate may also be referred to as the "required rate of return.")

Choosing a hurdle rate is similar to choosing a discount rate, in that it depends on risk. A firm's WACC is often used as the hurdle rate for projects that are roughly as risky as the firm's ongoing operations, with higher hurdle rates being used for riskier projects and lower hurdle rates being used for less risky projects.

Whenever the IRR for a project is lower than the hurdle rate, we reject the project. Any project with IRR greater than the hurdle rate merits further consideration. With enough capital to pursue all projects we're considering, we'd accept any project with IRR greater than the hurdle rate. If we have insufficient capital to pursue all such projects, we would calculate the NPV of each project and pursue the combination of projects that provides the highest total NPV.

Pros and Cons of Using IRR

One benefit of calculating the IRR for a project is that it's a relatively easy concept to explain to people without a finance background: it's the expected rate of return for the project. All else being equal, higher is better. That's relatively easy to grasp.

Along with NPV, IRR is generally regarded as the best method for evaluating projects/investments. (And it is therefore the most used method, along with NPV.)

NPV is generally considered a better evaluation method than IRR though, because NPV actually shows us how much value we're adding to the firm. If two projects are mutually exclusive due to budget limitations or other operational reasons, we want the one with the greater NPV, not the one with the greater IRR.

EXAMPLE: Beta Broadcasting is evaluating the following four projects. Beta has $500,000 of available capital.

	Initial Outlay	IRR	NPV
Project A	$300,000	18%	$80,000
Project B	$100,000	12%	$11,000
Project C	$100,000	13%	$13,000
Project D	$60,000	14%	$10,000

Beta should pursue projects A, B, and C. Even though Project D has a higher IRR than Projects B or C, it does not add as much total value. And because of the $500,000 total capital budget, we cannot pursue Project D without eliminating one of the other three projects.

Another disadvantage of IRR is that it is sometimes impossible to even calculate an IRR for a project if it has a particularly irregular series of cash flows (e.g., one that switches often between positive and negative cash flows). Or sometimes there could even be multiple IRRs for such a series of cash flows (i.e., multiple discount rates that would set the net present value to zero).

One final drawback of IRR is that it assumes that all cash flows from the project are reinvested at the same rate of return as the initial investment. In many cases, that's not actually possible.

Payback Period and Discounted Payback Period

Another way to evaluate a project is to calculate its "payback period." A project's payback period is the length of time until the after-tax inflows from the project exceed the initial outlay. Evaluating via payback period is essentially asking: how long until we break even?

EXAMPLE: Beta Broadcasting is evaluating a project with an initial cost of $200,000. The project is expected to provide after-tax cash flow of $50,000 per year. What is the payback period for this project?

In this case, because the cash inflows from the project are forecasted to be steady, we can simply divide the initial outlay by the annual cash flow to see how many years it would take to break even.

Payback period = $200,000 ÷ $50,000 per year

Payback period = 4 years

If the forecasted cash flows from a project are irregular, we have to manually add them up until we achieve payback.

EXAMPLE: Beta Broadcasting is evaluating a project with an initial cost of $200,000. The project is expected to provide the following after-tax cash flows. What is the payback period for this project?

Year 1	$30,000
Year 2	$70,000
Year 3	$100,000
Year 4	$200,000

The payback period for this project is 3 years, because that is the point by which Beta will have recouped its initial outlay ($30,000 + $70,000 + $100,000 = $200,000).

A major drawback of evaluating a project based on its payback period is that doing so ignores time value of money. Every cash flow is simply included in the calculation at its face value, regardless of how far in the future it occurs.

For this reason, it's common to calculate a *discounted* payback period for a project. The discounted payback period is the length of time until *discounted* after-tax cash flows exceed the initial outlay.

EXAMPLE: Beta Broadcasting is evaluating a project that has the following forecasted after-tax cash flows. The PV of each cash flow is shown in the adjacent column. What is the discounted payback period for the project?

	Cash Flow	**PV of Cash Flow**
Initial outlay	($290,000)	($290,000)
Year 1	$30,000	$27,273
Year 2	$70,000	$57,851
Year 3	$100,000	$75,131
Year 4	$200,000	$136,603

By the end of year 3, Beta has recouped $160,255 in discounted cash flows ($27,273 + $57,851 + $75,131). By the end of year 4, Beta has recouped $296,858 of discounted cash flows. Conclusion: Beta's discounted payback period for this project is just under 4 years.

Pros and Cons of Using Payback Period

The biggest benefit of evaluating investments based on their payback period is that payback period is very easy to calculate and understand.

If management is especially concerned about liquidity and risk, payback period gives useful information. For instance, if a project has a payback period of, say, 10 years, management might choose to eliminate the project from consideration without need for further evaluation. The idea behind such a decision would be that 10 years is simply too far in the future—too distant to feel very confident in the forecasts (and therefore in the success of the project).

A major *drawback* of evaluating projects based on either payback period or discounted payback period calculations is that doing so completely ignores any cash flows that occur after payback is achieved.

EXAMPLE: Beta Broadcasting is evaluating two projects: Project A and Project B. The two projects would require identical initial outlays. Each project is expected to achieve payback after three years. Project A, however, would continue to provide positive cash flow for another ten years after that, whereas Project B's cash flow would terminate shortly after three years. Project A is far preferable to project B, but if Beta only looks at payback period, it won't have any way of knowing that.

Still, despite its limitations, payback period is easy to calculate and easy to understand, so managers and financial professionals do use it frequently.

Profitability Index

The "profitability index" of an investment is the ratio of the present value of the project's cash inflows to the present value of the project's cash ouproftflows. That is,

$$\text{profitability index} \quad = \quad \frac{\text{PV of inflows}}{\text{PV of outflows}}$$

Profitability index is basically just a spin on the net present value concept, in that we are again comparing the present value of inflows to the present value of outflows. In this case though we are calculating the ratio of the one to the other rather than finding the difference between them. With profitability index, we are particularly concerned with whether the index is greater than one (i.e., the PV of inflows exceeds the PV of outflows). If the profitability index is greater than one, we also know that the project has a positive NPV (because PV of inflows exceeds PV of outflows).

In general, profitability index is not the most useful calculation. If we have already calculated that a project has a positive NPV, we already know that it has a profitability index greater than one. And when choosing between projects, we generally want to choose based on NPV (i.e., choosing the combination of projects that adds the greatest total value for investors) rather than by profitability index.

Chapter 8 Simple Summary

- The internal rate of return (IRR) of an investment is the discount rate at which the present value of the inflows is equal to the present value of the outflows. It is essentially the annual compounded rate of return for the investment.

- The hurdle rate is a rate of return target, set by management. If the anticipated IRR from a project is less than the hurdle rate, the project should be rejected.

- A project's payback period is the length of time it takes for the project's cash inflows to equal the outflows up to that point. Discounted payback period is a similar metric, except it instead uses the present value of cash flows instead of their face value.

- A major drawback of evaluating projects based on payback period is that doing so completely ignores any cash flow that occurs after payback is achieved.

- An investment's profitability index is the ratio of the present value of the investment's cash inflows to the present value of the investment's cash outflows.

PART THREE

The Investor's Perspective

CHAPTER NINE

Bond Valuation

As discussed in Chapter 1, the par value of a bond (also referred to as the bond's face value) is the value that the borrower must pay back upon maturity, and it is also the value upon which the interest payments are calculated.

The bond's "coupon rate" is the rate used to calculate periodic interest payments. Specifically, the interest paid per year will be equal to the bond's par value, multiplied by the bond's coupon rate.

EXAMPLE: A bond has a $1,000 par value and a 6% coupon rate. The bond will pay $60 of interest per year (i.e., $1,000 x 0.06).

If the bond pays interest semi-annually, the interest payment would be $30 every 6 months. (The coupon rate is stated on an annual basis. If the bond pays interest twice each year, each payment is half of the annual coupon.)

In many cases—for reasons we'll discuss momentarily—the *price* of a bond will be different from its face value. If you were considering buying a bond, you wouldn't just want to know the coupon rate. You would want to know how the amount of interest the bond pays compares to the price you'd actually have to pay to buy the bond. In that case, you could look at the bond's "current yield," which is calculated as the annual coupon payment divided by the current price.

$$\text{Current yield} \; = \; \frac{\text{Annual coupon}}{\text{Price}}$$

EXAMPLE: A bond has a $1,000 par value and a 6% coupon rate. The bond will pay $60 of interest per year (i.e., $1,000 x 0.06). The bond is currently selling for $960. What is the bond's current yield?

The bond's current yield is 6.25% (i.e., $60 annual coupon divided by the $960 price). Note that the bond's current yield is higher than its coupon rate, because the bond is selling for less than face value. (The lower the price an investor would have to pay for a bond, the higher the current yield. If the current price is less than the bond's face value, the current yield will be greater than the coupon rate.)

An even better method for evaluating a bond is to look at its "yield to maturity" (YTM). Yield to maturity is the rate of return that an investor would earn if she buys the bond at today's price, holds the bond to maturity, and receives all the promised payments on time (i.e., there's no default).

As with calculating internal rate of return, calculating YTM manually would be extremely time consuming, so most people use Excel or other similar tools.[1]

EXAMPLE: A three-year bond has a $1,000 par value and a 6% coupon rate, with interest paid semiannually ($30 every 6 months). The bond is currently selling for $960. The bond's YTM works out to 7.514%.

Again, note that the bond's YTM is higher than the coupon rate, because the bond is selling for less than its face value. (That is, the less a buyer has to pay in order to receive a given amount of future payments, the higher the buyer's rate of return.)

Bond Credit Risk Premium

Much like a person has a credit score that assesses the person's ability to repay a lender, businesses have credit ratings that assess the same thing. These ratings are provided by credit rating agencies. Moody's, Standard and Poor's, and Fitch are the three largest such agencies.

As we discussed in Chapter 1, borrowers with a lower credit rating (i.e., a higher chance of

---

[1] See obliviousinvestor.com/excel-finance/ for a discussion of using Excel to calculate YTM.

default) have to pay higher interest rates than borrowers with better credit ratings.

From the perspective of the lender, that higher interest rate means a higher rate of return. That is, lending to higher-risk borrowers offers a "risk premium" (i.e., a higher expected rate of return) relative to lending to lower-risk borrowers.

Treasury bonds carry essentially no risk of default and therefore offer the lowest interest rates.

"Investment-grade bonds" are bonds issued by borrowers that have good credit ratings and therefore a low risk of default. They are, however, still riskier than Treasury bonds and therefore offer a higher rate of interest (a risk premium).

"Junk bonds" (also known as "high-yield bonds") are those from issuers who have credit ratings that are below investment grade. Due to their high risk, junk bonds offer an even greater risk premium than investment grade bonds.

On the following page are the ratings tables (i.e., possible credit ratings) from the three major bond rating agencies. Note the distinction between investment-grade and non-investment-grade (i.e., junk bonds).

	Moody's	S&P	Fitch
Investment grade	Aaa	AAA	AAA
	Aa1	AA+	AA+
	Aa2	AA	AA
	Aa3	AA-	AA-
	A1	A+	A+
	A2	A	A
	A3	A-	A-
	Baa1	BBB+	BBB+
	Baa2	BBB	BBB
	Baa3	BBB-	BBB-
Non-investment grade ("junk")	Ba1	BB+	BB+
	Ba2	BB	BB
	Ba3	BB-	BB-
	B1	B+	B+
	B2	B	B
	B3	B-	B-
	Caa1	CCC+	CCC+
	Caa2	CCC	CCC
	Caa3	CCC-	CCC-
	Ca	CC	CC
	C	C	C

Bond Pricing

Instead of holding a bond all the way until it matures, it's also possible for a bondholder to sell the bond to another investor, so that it is the new owner who collects interest payments going forward, as well as the repayment of principal upon maturity.

In such a case, how would the buyer choose how much to offer for the bond? In short, by doing a present value calculation. The value of a bond at any point in time is simply the sum of the present values of all of the cash flows from the bond (i.e., the present value of the interest payments plus the present value of the principal payment upon maturity).

As you will recall from Chapters 6 and 7, the appropriate discount rate to use in a present value calculation is the rate of return that would be available from other investments with a similar level of risk. So, when calculating the present value of a bond, the appropriate discount rate is the YTM that investors could currently earn from other bonds with similar maturity and credit rating.

EXAMPLE: Seven years ago, you bought a 10-year Treasury bond. From the perspective of a potential buyer, your bond is essentially a 3-year Treasury bond (because the maturity date is now just three years away). If new 3-year Treasury bonds are currently offering a 4% yield to maturity, other investors would only be willing to buy your bond if it too offered a 4% rate of return. So they would use a 4% discount rate when calculating the present value of your bond.

Prevailing interest rates in the market change over time. But the amount of interest that a given bond pays does not change. So the market value of the bond must change in order for it to offer the same yield to maturity as other bonds of similar risk.

Sometimes the bond's market price will be greater than its face value, in which case the bond is said to be "selling at a premium." This happens when the bond's coupon rate is greater than the YTM currently offered by other bonds of similar risk.

Other times the bond's market price will be less than its face value, in which case the bond is said to be "selling at a discount." This happens when the bond's coupon rate is less than the YTM currently offered by other bonds of similar risk.

In short, a bond will sell at a premium or discount whenever its coupon rate is different from the applicable market interest rate. And the premium or discount will be set (i.e., the price of the bond will be adjusted) so that the bond's YTM is equal to the applicable market interest rate (i.e., equal to the YTM available from similar bonds).

EXAMPLE: You own a $1,000 Treasury bond, with five years remaining until maturity and a 5% coupon rate. 5-year Treasury bonds are currently yielding 4% (YTM). Because your bond has a higher coupon rate than the YTM available on similar bonds, it will sell at a premium.

The premium increases the cost to an investor who buys your bond—with the result being that the investor will earn a lower return than if there were no premium. And that's exactly the point. The point of the premium is to reduce the yield to maturity (i.e., rate of return) so that it's equal to the YTM from similar bonds.

EXAMPLE: You own a $1,000 Treasury bond, with five years remaining until maturity and a 3% coupon rate. 5-year Treasury bonds are currently yielding 5% (YTM). Because your bond has a lower coupon rate than the YTM available on similar bonds, it will sell at a discount.

The discount reduces the cost to an investor who buys your bond—with the result being that the investor will earn a higher return than if there were no discount. And, again, that's exactly the point. The point of the discount is to increase the yield to maturity (i.e., rate of return) so that it's equal to the YTM from similar bonds.

To summarize, bond prices and market interest rates have an inverse relationship. When interest rates go up, bond prices go down. And when interest rates go down, bond prices go up. There are two ways to try to make sense of this phenomenon, but they're really just two ways of saying the same thing.

1. As we discussed earlier in the chapter, the value of a bond is simply the present value of all of the bond's cash flows. So when market interest rates go up, bonds' present values will be calculated using higher discount rates. A higher discount rate means a lower present value (i.e., lower price). And, conversely, when interest rates go down, bond

present values will be calculated with a lower discount rate, with the result being a higher present value (i.e., higher price).

2. When market interest rates go up, nobody will buy an existing bond with its lower coupon rate, unless that bond is sold at a lower price. And when interest rates go down, existing bonds with their higher coupon rates become more valuable—their prices go up.

Bond Maturity Risk Premium

Longer-term bonds (i.e., those with maturity dates further in the future) carry greater "interest rate risk" than shorter-term bonds. That is, longer-term bonds experience a greater degree of price fluctuation due to changes in market interest rates than shorter-term bonds do.

The reason for this greater price sensitivity is that, when doing a present value calculation, a change in the discount rate has a larger effect for cash flows further in the future. So the further in the future a bond's cash flows will be received, the more its present value (i.e., market price) will fluctuate when the discount rate (i.e., the applicable market interest rate) changes.

Because longer-term bonds are riskier than shorter-term bonds, longer-term bonds usually carry a higher rate of interest (i.e., they offer a risk premium, relative to bonds with shorter maturities).

A yield curve is a chart that shows the interest rates for bonds of equal credit quality and varying maturity dates. For example, the chart below shows the yield curve for Treasury bonds as of this writing in October 2020.

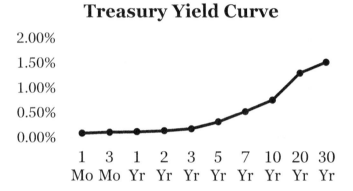

Treasury Yield Curve

There are exceptions, but in most circumstances, a yield curve will be upward sloping (i.e., showing higher interest rates for longer-term bonds than for shorter-term bonds). This is essentially a graphic representation of the risk premium that investors usually demand for longer-term bonds.

Chapter 9 Simple Summary

- A bond's yield to maturity is the rate of return that an investor would earn if they bought the bond today and held it until maturity (with no defaults occurring).

- Investors demand a risk premium for credit risk. That is, the lower a bond's credit rating, the higher its yield to maturity will generally be.

- A bond's market price is the sum of the present values of each of the bond's cash flows (i.e., interest payments and principal), discounted using the YTM that would be available from other similar bonds.

- When market interest rates go up, prices of existing bonds go down. When market interest rates go down, prices of existing bonds go up.

- Longer-term bonds have greater price sensitivity to market interest rate changes.

- Yield curves are usually upward sloping. That is, investors generally demand a risk premium for longer-term bonds because they are riskier.

CHAPTER TEN

Stock Valuation

In the previous chapter we discussed the fact that the market price of a bond is simply the net present value of the bond's cash flows. In theory, the same is true for a stock: the value of a share of stock is the sum of the present values of the cash flows that will come from the stock.

But we immediately run into two problems if we try to implement such a concept in real life.

First, we don't know what cash flows the stock will provide. How much will the stock pay in dividends, and on which dates in the future? And how much would an investor be able to sell the stock for at a later time? We don't know.

Second, what discount rate should we use? We don't know exactly what rate of return is available from other similarly-risky investments, since we don't know what returns other stocks will provide.

The finance industry has, therefore, developed various models for trying to value stocks in the face of such uncertainty.

Dividend Discount Model

The dividend discount model essentially assumes that the firm in question will continue operating indefinitely, and the investor in question will continue to hold the stock indefinitely. In such a case, the present value of the stock is just the present value of the future dividends.

To calculate the present value of such dividends, we can use the formula for present value of a "perpetuity." A perpetuity is an annuity that pays a fixed amount of income, indefinitely. (Imagine a bond that never matures—it just keeps paying interest every year, forever.) Perpetuities aren't very common in the real world. However, they're useful as a model for stocks.

The present value of a perpetuity with fixed payments is calculated as the amount of the payment, divided by the discount rate. So for a stock with constant (unchanging) dividends, the present value of the stock would be calculated as follows:

$$\text{Present value} = \frac{\text{Annual dividend}}{\text{Discount rate}}$$

EXAMPLE: A stock pays a steady annual dividend of $10 per share. Using an 8% discount rate, what is the stock's present value, according to the dividend discount model?

The stock's present value is $125, calculated as the annual dividend ($10.00), divided by the discount rate (0.08).

83

For a perpetuity with income that *increases* over time, the present value is calculated as *next* year's payment, divided by the difference between the discount rate and the rate at which the income from the perpetuity is growing. Therefore, for a stock with dividends that are assumed to grow by a steady percentage each year, the value of the stock would be calculated as follows:

$$\text{PV} = \frac{\text{Next year's dividend}}{\text{Discount rate} - \text{dividend growth rate}}$$

EXAMPLE: A stock's dividends are growing at a steady rate of 3% per year. This year, the stock paid a $4.00 annual dividend. Given an 8% discount rate, what is the stock's present value according to the dividend discount model?

If the stock paid a $4.00 dividend this year, and its dividends are growing at a 3% rate, next year's dividend will be $4.12. So the present value would be $82.40, calculated as follows:

$$\text{Present value} = \frac{\$4.12}{0.08 - 0.03} = \$82.40$$

At this point you may be wondering, "what about stocks that don't pay any dividends?" And that's a great point. A dividend-based model is particularly dubious when valuing a firm that isn't currently paying any dividends, because the analyst would be forced to guess *when* the firm would start paying dividends, as well as how much it would pay. For such firms, earnings-based or asset-based approaches are often used instead.

Earnings-Based Valuation

Some firms can be profitable, yet pay no dividends. A typical approach in such cases is to value the firm based on its earnings.

"Earnings per common share"—often just referred to as earnings per share (EPS)—is the ratio of the firm's net income, minus any preferred dividends, to the average number of common shares outstanding over the course of the year.

$$\text{EPS} = \frac{\text{Net income} - \text{Preferred dividends}}{\text{Average common shares outstanding}}$$

We back out preferred dividends because we only want to know how much income is available to common stockholders when calculating earnings per common share.

A firm's "price-to-earnings ratio" (often just "PE ratio") is the ratio of the price per share of common stock to the firm's earnings per share.

$$\text{Price-to-earnings ratio} = \frac{\text{Price per share}}{\text{Earnings per share}}$$

PE ratio shows how much the market is willing to pay for the firm relative to its current earnings.

Generally, the higher the firm's anticipated growth, the greater the price that investors will be willing to pay per dollar of current earnings (because investors are assuming that future earnings will be much higher than current earnings).

Risk also a factor. Investors prefer (i.e., will pay more for) more predictable earnings than for less predictable earnings. As such, all else being equal, riskier firms will have lower PE ratios than less risky firms.

A stock can be valued by trying to find an appropriate PE ratio for the firm in question, by looking at the PE ratios of comparable firms. (The most ideal benchmark would be the PE ratio for another firm in the same industry, with similar growth prospects and with a similar risk level.) Then once an appropriate PE has been determined, we can value the stock by multiplying that PE ratio by the firm's earnings per share.

EXAMPLE: A firm has an earnings per share of $3.00. A competing, very similar firm has a PE ratio of 15. Using that PE ratio as a benchmark, a fair value for this firm's stock would be $45 per share.

Asset-Based Valuation

An alternative to dividend- or earnings-based calculations is to take an asset-based approach to valuing a stock. That is, what is the amount by which the firm's assets exceed its liabilities, after stating each at their fair market value (as opposed to their accounting/book value)? This is basically what the firm would be worth if the owners decided to cease operations immediately and liquidate everything. As a result, this valuation is most useful as a "floor." That is, a firm should never be worth less than this amount, and firms are often worth more than this amount because continuing operations is *usually* more profitable than ceasing operations and liquidating the firm's assets.

Capital Asset Pricing Model (CAPM)

In any present value calculation, we need to know what discount rate to use. The proper discount rate is generally the expected return from other investments with a similar level of risk. When doing a present value calculation for a stock (e.g., when using the dividend discount model), that would mean we would want to use the expected return from similarly-risky stocks. But how do we determine that?

The classic answer in the field of finance is the capital asset pricing model (CAPM). CAPM states that the expected return for a given stock consists of two components:

1. The rate of return that an investor could currently earn from a risk-free investment, plus
2. A risk premium (i.e., some additional return to compensate the investor for the fact that the stock is risky).

Of course, no investment is *completely* risk-free. In practice though, the interest rate on short-term Treasury bonds ("T-Bills") is often used as the risk-free rate, given that they have essentially no default risk and very little price volatility.

And the risk premium for the stock is calculated as the market risk premium, multiplied by the firm's "beta."

The market risk premium is the risk premium that the overall stock market is expected to earn relative to the risk-free rate of return. (That is, it's the market's expected return, minus the risk-free rate.)

A stock's "beta" (β) is a measure of how risky (volatile) the stock is as compared to the overall stock market. The overall market has a beta of 1. A stock that is twice as risky as the overall market would have a beta of 2, while a stock that is half as risky as the market would have a beta of 0.5.[1]

To summarize, CAPM states that:

$$ER = R_F + \beta (ER_M - R_F)$$

---

[1] A relevant point here is that we're not including any risk that accrues simply from having an undiversified portfolio. For example, a portfolio that consists of just one stock will be riskier than the market overall, even if the stock itself is not an especially risky stock. But that's not what beta is concerned with. Beta is only concerned with how the risk level of an already-diversified portfolio would be affected by including the stock in question.

Chapter 10 Simple Summary

- The dividend discount model values a stock by calculating the net present value of the stock's future dividends.

- Stocks can also be valued based on their earnings—for instance by finding the PE ratios for other similar firms and multiplying the average of those PE ratios by the firm's own earnings per share.

- It can sometimes be informative to determine an asset-based valuation for a firm, calculated as the fair value of the firm's assets minus the fair value of the firm's liabilities. This amount is essentially what the firm would be worth if operations were ceased and the firm's assets were liquidated.

- According to the capital asset pricing model (CAPM), a stock's expected return is the risk-free rate of return, plus a premium to account for the stock's risk.

- A stock's beta is a measure of how risky it is. A stock that is riskier than the overall stock market will have a beta greater than one, while a stock that is less risky than the overall market will have a beta less than one.

CHAPTER ELEVEN

Efficient Markets

You may have noticed in Chapter 9 that, when discussing bond pricing, it was taken as a given that a bond's market price *would* be equal to the net present value of its cash flows. How does that happen? It's not as if there's any regulation of the bond market that insists that bonds must be bought and sold at such a price.

It happens because the bond market is generally quite "efficient." An efficient market is one in which assets are bought and sold at prices that reflect their fair value, given all currently available information.

For instance, to use the bond market as an example again, if you own a Treasury bond and you want to sell it, you have essentially no hope of selling the bond for more than its fair value. There are so many other sellers in the marketplace, so many Treasury bonds being sold, and information about Treasury bonds is so freely available, that nobody will buy your overpriced bond. Investors looking to buy Treasury bonds will instead buy from sellers who are selling at fair value.

Similarly, if you are looking to *buy* a Treasury bond, it's extremely unlikely that you'll find anybody willing to sell you one at a price lower than fair value. After all, why would anybody sell to you at such a price, when there are plenty of other buyers who would be willing to pay fair value?

Contrast the market for Treasury bonds with the market for homes in a particular area. In a given neighborhood, there are usually not very many homes up for sale at any given moment. And the number of potential buyers is limited as well. In addition, the homes in a given area tend not to be identical to each other—each one is unique in its own ways, making it harder to compare one to another. As such, it can sometimes be possible to find a buyer who will overpay for a given home, or a seller who will sell for less than what their home is likely worth. Housing markets are much less efficient than the market for Treasury bonds.

Price Changes and New Information

The more efficient a market, the faster it responds to new information. For example, if a rating agency reduces the credit rating of a given corporation from AAA to BBB, prices for bonds issued by that corporation will usually change very quickly. Specifically, the prices of such bonds would move downward to reflect the higher rate of risk. The bonds' prices would move downward until the bonds offered an expected rate of return equal to that of BBB-rated bonds with similar duration.

Again, contrast this with the less-efficient nature of a housing market. Imagine that a large corporation announces that it will be opening a new facility in a given area, creating several thousand new jobs. Would everybody in the area who is currently trying to sell a home immediately respond by adjusting their list price upward, to account for the new higher level of demand for housing? No. In fact, many would-be sellers probably wouldn't adjust their list prices at all. This is another way that we can see the difference between an efficient market and an inefficient market: inefficient markets respond slowly (or in some cases, not at all) to new information.

Stock Market Efficiency

The extent to which the stock market is or isn't efficient is a topic of much discussion in the financial industry. It's an important topic because, if the market were perfectly efficient, then there would be no point in trying to find underpriced stocks (i.e., stocks that will earn above-average returns for their level of risk). A stock investor's best bet would simply be to buy a mutual fund or ETF that tracks the overall market at a very low cost.

It's difficult to say exactly how efficient the stock market is. For all the reasons discussed in the previous chapter, it's hard to determine the appropriate valuation for a stock. So there's no easy way to simply look at current stock prices and see if they match their intrinsic values. That is, there is disagreement about how efficient the stock market is or isn't, in large part because people disagree about what an efficient stock market would look like in the first place.

One thing we can say confidently is that the stock market is at least efficiency-*seeking*. That is, inefficiencies tend to disappear once they become known. For instance, if it becomes well known that stocks that have a given set of characteristics tend to be underpriced, more investors will buy those stocks, thereby driving up their prices until they're no longer underpriced.

In short, mispricings are difficult to find reliably, because 1) they're usually eliminated once they are found and 2) there are many thousands of well-funded professional investors (as well as many amateurs) trying to find them.

Expectations Are "Priced In"

At any given time, the price of a stock reflects the market's consensus expectations about the company's future earnings and dividends.

For example, if the market expects Amazon to have rapid earnings growth going forward, then Amazon shares will be expensive relative to companies with lower expected future earnings (i.e.,

Amazon will have a higher PE ratio). One would say that the market's expectations about Amazon's earnings growth are "priced in" (i.e., they're already built into the price).

This is a key point to understand because it means that if the company's earnings grow quickly, but no more quickly than the market expected them to, the stock's performance will probably not be any better than the performance of the rest of the market (and will probably be worse).

In other words, the performance of a given stock is not determined by whether the underlying company performs well or poorly. Rather, it is determined by whether the underlying company does better or worse *than the market expected it to do.*

Chapter 11 Simple Summary

- An efficient market is one in which assets are bought and sold at prices that reflect their actual value, given all currently available information.

- In an efficient market, prices will change quickly in response to new information.

- The market's expectations about each firm's future earnings and dividends are "priced in" (i.e., they're already built into the price of that firm's stock).

Accessing and Deploying Capital

Corporate finance examines the ways in which businesses access capital and deploy capital. And the most critical role of financial markets is to connect providers of capital (investors) with users of capital (businesses).

Accessing Capital

When a business wants to raise additional capital, it has two options: borrow money or sell equity (i.e., sell a share of the business). Each option comes with a cost to the firm. With borrowing, the cost is the interest that the firm will have to pay to the lender(s). With the sale of equity, the cost is the result of the fact that the existing owners will get a smaller share of dividends going forward—and they will have a smaller share of the other shareholder rights as well (e.g., voting rights).

Borrowing—either via issuing bonds or taking out a loan with a bank or other lender—has the advantage of being less costly than selling equity (in most normal circumstances, at least). The downside of borrowing is that it is risky, because it creates a legal obligation to pay the lender(s) on time. And that obligation can be a challenge to meet if the business does not have sufficient cash flow.

Selling equity is less risky than borrowing, because the firm has no *obligation* to pay dividends to shareholders. It is, however, more expensive than borrowing, because investors will demand a higher expected rate of return for stock investments than for bond investments, given the uncertainty involved (i.e., given that they are not receiving a contractual guarantee of a certain amount of payment on certain dates, as they would receive with bond investments).

A key point here is that the very thing that makes selling equity *less* risky from the perspective of the firm (i.e., the fact that there is no fixed obligation to pay) is the thing that makes equity *more* risky than bonds from the perspective of the investor. And this riskiness from the point of view of the investor is the reason that stocks carry higher expected returns than bonds (and are therefore more costly from the perspective of the firm raising capital).

A firm has one final source of capital: its own profits. Earnings that are not distributed to shareholders as a dividend can be reinvested in the company. Whether a firm chooses to reinvest earnings or distribute them as a dividend generally depends on the rate of return that management thinks it can earn on reinvested earnings. If management thinks it can earn a higher rate of return for a given level of risk than is available elsewhere, it should retain the earnings rather than distribute them. (This is one reason why newer, faster-growing firms often do not pay dividends even if they are profitable.)

Deploying Capital

Capital budgeting is the process of evaluating potential ways in which a business can *use* its capital. When evaluating a project, the first step is to forecast the related cash flows, making sure, in the process, to look only at relevant cash flows (ignoring sunk costs, for instance).

A critical point when evaluating the cash flows from a project is to consider time value of money (i.e., the fact that a dollar received sooner is more valuable than a dollar received later). We do this by calculating the present value of each cash flow (i.e., the amount that a future cash flow is worth today). When calculating the present value of a cash flow, it is important to use a discount rate that reflects the rate of return that could be earned from other investments with a similar level of risk.

Generally, the best way to evaluate a potential project or investment is to calculate its net present value (NPV), which is the sum of the present values of each cash flow (both inflows and outflows) related to the project. A project with a positive NPV adds value for shareholders (assuming that the project ultimately performs as forecasted), whereas projects with a negative NPV subtract value. An ideal capital budgeting approach is to select the combination of projects that provides the greatest total NPV without exceeding the available budget.

Another common capital budgeting method is to calculate the expected internal rate of return of a project (i.e., the compounded rate of return that the project is expected to earn). If the expected IRR is below the hurdle rate set by management, the project should be rejected.

The Investor's Perspective

Again, the most important role of financial markets is to connect providers of capital (investors) with users of capital (businesses). And it is often informative to consider topics not only from the perspective of the firm but from the perspective of the investor as well.

In an efficient financial market:

- Prices should respond quickly to new information,
- A given financial instrument (e.g., a stock or a bond) should generally have an expected

return that corresponds to the instrument's types and levels of risk, and

• The market price of a financial instrument should, in most cases, represent the present value of all the future payments that are anticipated to come from the instrument.

For a bond, it is relatively straightforward to calculate the present value, because we know what the anticipated payments are, and we know what discount rate to use (i.e., the yield-to-maturity from other bonds with similar levels of risk).

For a stock, given how challenging it is to predict with any accuracy what the future payments will be, the present value is a very rough estimate, as would be any calculation of expected return.

A Final Thought

One final reminder: in finance, unlike in accounting, there is no official set of rules that must be followed. The focus is instead on doing any type of analysis that you think will be helpful when making the decisions you have to make.

APPENDIX

Financial Ratios

Author's note: this appendix is an adapted chapter from my book *Accounting Made Simple*.

Suppose that we're looking at a firm's balance sheet, with the goal of assessing the firm's short-term solvency (i.e., the firm's ability to pay its bills in the near future). We would naturally look at the firm's cash balance and other current asset accounts. But we wouldn't stop there. The information we need is not simply how much the firm has in current assets, but rather how that amount *compares to the firm's current liabilities*. We want to know a ratio.

Ratios (rather than simply dollar amounts) also make it easier to compare firms of different size. For example, if one firm has a cash balance of $10 million and another has a cash balance of $100 million, which firm will have an easier time paying its bills over the next three months? We don't know—until we get more information. Again, we need to know how each firm's cash balance compares to the firm's liabilities. We want to know a ratio.

In this chapter we'll discuss various ratios that assess a firm's liquidity, profitability, leverage, and efficiency. To be clear, the ratios described in this chapter are just some of the most commonly used ones. There are many more that are not discussed here. (Again, a neat point about financial analysis is that you can do whatever calculations you think are relevant to inform the decision you are making.)

Liquidity Ratios

Liquidity ratios are used to determine how easily a company will be able to meet its short-term financial obligations. The most frequently used liquidity ratio is known as the current ratio:

$$\text{Current ratio} = \frac{\text{Current assets}}{\text{Current liabilities}}$$

A company's current ratio provides an assessment of the company's ability to pay off its current liabilities (liabilities due within a year or less) using its current assets (cash and assets likely to be converted to cash within a year or less).

"Net working capital" is a closely-related metric for assessing a firm's short-term solvency. In this case though, it is not a ratio. Rather, it is the difference between current assets and current liabilities.

$$\text{Net working capital} = \text{Current assets} - \text{Current liabilities}$$

Quick ratio is yet another metric that seeks to assess the company's ability to pay off its current liabilities.

$$\text{Quick ratio} = \frac{\text{Current assets} - \text{Inventory}}{\text{Current liabilities}}$$

The difference between quick ratio and current ratio is that the calculation of quick ratio excludes inventory balances from the numerator. This is done in order to provide a worst-case-scenario assessment: how well will the company be able to fulfill its current liabilities if sales are slow (that is, if inventories are not converted to cash)?

EXAMPLE: ABC Toys (see balance sheet on the following page) would calculate its liquidity ratios as follows:

$$\text{Current ratio} = \frac{40,000 + 100,000 + 60,000}{50,000 + 150,000} = 1$$

$$\text{Quick ratio} = \frac{40,000 + 60,000}{50,000 + 150,000} = 0.5$$

A current ratio of 1 tells us that ABC Toys' current assets match its current liabilities, meaning it shouldn't have any trouble handling its financial obligations over the next 12 months.

However, a quick ratio of only 0.5 indicates that ABC Toys will need to maintain at least some level of sales in order to satisfy its liabilities.

Balance Sheet, ABC Toys	
Assets	
Cash and Cash Equivalents	$40,000
Inventory	100,000
Accounts Receivable	60,000
Property, Plant, and Equipment	300,000
Total Assets	500,000
Liabilities	
Accounts Payable	50,000
Income Tax Payable	150,000
Total Liabilities	200,000
Owners' Equity	
Common Stock	160,000
Retained Earnings	140,000
Total Owners' Equity	300,000
Total Liabilities + Owners' Equity	$500,000

Profitability Ratios

While a company's net income is certainly a valuable piece of information, it doesn't tell the whole story in terms of how profitable a company really is. For example, Amazon's net income is going to absolutely dwarf the net income of your favorite local

Italian restaurant. But the two businesses are of such different sizes that the comparison is rather meaningless. That's why we use the two following ratios:

$$\text{Return on assets} = \frac{\text{Net income}}{\text{Assets}}$$

$$\text{Return on equity} = \frac{\text{Net income}}{\text{Owners' equity}}$$

A company's return on assets (ROA) shows us the company's profitability in comparison to the company's size (as measured by total assets). In other words, return on assets seeks to answer the question, "How efficiently is this company using its assets to generate profits?"

Return on equity (ROE) is similar except that shareholders' equity is used in place of total assets. Return on equity asks, "How efficiently is this company using its investors' money to generate profits?"[1]

By using return on assets or return on equity, you can actually make meaningful comparisons between the profitability of two companies, even if the companies are of very different sizes.

---

[1] It is also common to calculate return on assets and return on equity using the average asset balance over the period and average owners' equity balance over the period, rather than the period-ending balances.

EXAMPLE: Using the previous balance sheet and the income statement below, we can calculate the following profitability ratios for ABC Toys:

$$\text{Return on assets } = \frac{90,000}{500,000} = 18\%$$

$$\text{Return on equity } = \frac{90,000}{300,000} = 30\%$$

Income Statement, ABC Toys	
Revenue	
Sales	$300,000
Cost of Goods Sold	(100,000)
Gross Profit	200,000
Expenses	
Rent	30,000
Salaries and Wages	80,000
Total Expenses	110,000
Net Income	$90,000

A company's gross profit margin shows what percentage of sales remains after covering the cost of the sold inventory. This gross profit is then used to cover overhead costs, with the remainder being the company's net income.

$$\text{Gross profit margin} = \frac{\text{Sales} - \text{Cost of goods sold}}{\text{Sales}}$$

EXAMPLE: Virginia runs a business selling cosmetics. Over the course of the year, her total sales were $80,000, and her cost of goods sold was $20,000. Virginia's gross profit margin for the year is 75%, calculated as follows:

$$\frac{\text{Sales} - \text{Cost of goods sold}}{\text{Sales}} = \frac{\$80,000 - \$20,000}{\$80,000}$$

Gross profit margin is often used to make comparisons between companies within an industry. For example, comparing the gross profit margin of two different grocery stores can give you an idea of which one does a better job of keeping inventory costs down.

Gross profit margin comparisons across different industries can be rather meaningless. For instance, a grocery store is going to have a lower profit margin than a software company, regardless of which company is run in a more cost-effective manner.

Financial Leverage Ratios

Financial leverage ratios show the extent to which a company has used debt (as opposed to capital from shareholders) to finance its operations.

107

A company's debt ratio shows what portion of a company's assets has been financed with debt.

$$\text{Debt ratio} \ = \ \frac{\text{Liabilities}}{\text{Assets}}$$

A company's debt-to-equity ratio shows the ratio of financing via debt to financing via capital from shareholders.[1]

$$\text{Debt-to-equity ratio} \ = \ \frac{\text{Liabilities}}{\text{Owners' equity}}$$

Asset Turnover Ratios

Asset turnover ratios seek to show how efficiently a company uses its assets. The two most commonly used turnover ratios are inventory turnover and accounts receivables turnover.

$$\text{Inventory turnover} \ = \ \frac{\text{Cost of goods sold}}{\text{Average inventory}}$$

The calculation of inventory turnover shows how many times a company's inventory is sold and replaced over the course of a period. The "average

---

[1] In many cases, the debt ratio and debt-to-equity ratio are calculated excluding accounts payable from the numerator. Sometimes they are calculated excluding *all* short-term liabilities from the numerator.

inventory" part of the equation is the average inventory balance over the period, calculated as follows:

$$\text{Average inventory} = \frac{\text{Beg. inventory} + \text{Ending inventory}}{2}$$

Inventory period shows how long, on average, inventory is on hand before it is sold.

$$\text{Inventory period} = \frac{365}{\text{Inventory turnover}}$$

A higher inventory turnover (and thus, a lower inventory period) shows that the company's inventory is selling quickly and is indicative that management is doing a good job of stocking products that are in demand.

A company's receivables turnover (calculated as credit sales over a period divided by average accounts receivable over the period) shows how quickly the company is collecting upon its accounts receivable.

$$\text{Receivables turnover} = \frac{\text{Credit sales}}{\text{Avg. accounts receivable}}$$

Average collection period is exactly what it sounds like: the average length of time that a receivable from a customer is outstanding prior to collection.

$$\text{Avg. collection period} = \frac{365}{\text{Receivables turnover}}$$

Obviously, higher receivables turnover and lower average collection period is generally the goal. If a company's average collection period steadily increases from one year to the next, it could be an indication that the company needs to address its policies in terms of when and to whom it extends credit when making a sale.

Simple Summary

- Liquidity ratios show how easily a company will be able to meet its short-term financial obligations. The two most common liquidity ratios are current ratio and quick ratio.

- Profitability ratios seek to analyze how profitable a company is in relation to its size. Return on assets, return on equity, and gross profit margin are frequently-used profitability ratios.

- Financial leverage ratios express to what extent a company is using debt (instead of shareholder investment) to finance its operations.

- Asset turnover ratios seek to show how efficiently a company uses its assets. Inventory turnover and receivables turnover are the most common turnover ratios.

Acknowledgements

As always, my thanks go to my editing team: Pat, Debbi, and Kalinda. Your feedback has once again resulted in a book that is far easier to understand than anything I could have produced on my own.

And thanks especially to Allan Roth who generously contributed his time and expertise to serve as technical editor. Allan, your feedback and support over the years—both on this project and others—means more to me than you know.

About the Author:

Mike is the author of several financial books as well as the popular blog ObliviousInvestor.com. He is a Missouri licensed CPA. Mike's writing has been featured in many places, including *The Wall Street Journal*, *Money*, *Forbes*, *MarketWatch*, and *Morningstar*.

Also by Mike Piper:

Accounting Made Simple: Accounting Explained in 100 Pages or Less

Cost Accounting Made Simple: Cost Accounting Explained in 100 Pages or Less

Microeconomics Made Simple: Basic Microeconomic Principles Explained in 100 Pages or Less

Taxes Made Simple: Income Taxes Explained in 100 Pages or Less

Investing Made Simple: Investing in Index Funds Explained in 100 Pages or Less

Independent Contractor, Sole Proprietor, and LLC Taxes Explained in 100 Pages or Less

LLC vs. S-Corp vs. C-Corp Explained in 100 Pages or Less

Can I Retire? Managing Your Retirement Savings Explained in 100 Pages or Less

Social Security Made Simple: Social Security Retirement Benefits and Related Planning Topics Explained in 100 Pages or Less

INDEX

Where:

ER = expected return of the stock in question

R_F = risk-free rate

β = beta of the stock in question

ER_M = expected return of the market

And in the above equation, "$ER_M - R_F$" represents the market risk premium, while "$\beta (ER_M - R_F)$" represents the stock in question's risk premium.

EXAMPLE: A stock has a beta of 0.6. The risk-free rate is currently 1%, and the stock market has an expected return of 8%. What is the stock's expected return, according to the capital asset pricing model?

$ER = R_F + \beta (ER_M - R_F)$

$ER = 1\% + 0.6 \text{ x } (8\% - 1\%)$

$ER = 1\% + 4.2\% = 5.2\%$

The stock's expected return is 5.2%, which represents a 4.2% risk premium relative to the risk-free rate. Of note, this risk premium is 60% of the 7% risk premium that the overall stock market is expected to earn. That is, the stock has a beta of 0.6, which means that the stock is 60% as risky as the overall market. So the stock's expected return includes a risk premium that is 60% of the overall market's risk premium.

Printed in Great Britain
by Amazon